THEY SHALL LAY HANDS ON THE SICK

GOD'S POWER TRANSMITTED
THROUGH YOUR HANDS....

AYODEJI DAVID OLUSANMI

COPYRIGHT

THEY SHALL LAY HANDS ON THE SICK
by Ayodeji David Olusanmi

Copyright ©2017 by Ayodeji David Olusanmi
ISBN: 978-1-945174-10-0

Contact Copyright Holder at
Ayodeji D. Olusanmi
Baruch Publishing
152 Oval Road North Dagenham,
Essex RM10 9EH
England

a.ilesanmi85@yahoo.co.uk

All Right Reserved. No part of this publication may be reproduced, stored in retrieval system, or transmitted in any form or by any means without the express written consent of copyright holder.

Unless otherwise noted, all Scripture quotations are taken from the King James Version of the Holy Bible, which is in the public domain.

Scripture noted AMP are taken from the Amplified Bible, Copyright ©1954, 1958, 1962, 1965, 1978 by The Lockman Foundation. All rights reserved.

Sciptures noted NLT are taken from the Holy Bible. New Living Translation copyright © 1996, 2004, 2007 by Tyndale House Foundation. All rights reserved.

APPRECIATION

We are to give honour to whom it is due. I would like to honour Dr Daniel K. Olukoya, the General Overseer of Mountain of Fire and Miracles Ministries Worldwide, for all he has done and is doing for me. Daddy, your impact in my life cannot be quantified. My wife and I love you. I thank God for giving me a place to serve in MFM. It is an honour to partake of your grace, Sir.

I would also like to honour Rev & Rev (Mrs) Olusola Areogun, the General Overseer of Life Oasis International Church (The Dream Centre). Daddy, Mummy, my wife and I are grateful for the words you have sown in our lives over the years and are so blessed that we have followed your ministry. My wife and I appreciate the wisdom that comes to us from you anytime we are privileged to meet you. We have always treasured those moments.

Furthermore, I would like to honour Pastor Tinu Olajide, Assistant Regional Overseer, Mountain of Fire and Miracle Ministries, Sweden & Finland as well. Firstly, for your constant spiritual/moral input and guidance into the life of my wife and I. Secondly, for taking time out to help edit, correct and proofread the manuscripts. Your input is appreciated.

Finally, I also all honour those who have been a blessing to me over the years. God will reward your labour of love.

Amen

DEDICATION

I DEDICATE THIS BOOK TO MY WIFE – MARGARET OLUWASEUN OLUSANMI – WHO HAS BEEN A TREMENDOUS INSPIRATION AND HELPER TO MY LIFE AND MINISTRY. INDEED, A HELPER SUITABLE FOR ME!

CONTENT

Intorduction

Chapter 1: The Doctrine of Laying on of Hands.

Chapter 2: Jesus Laid Hands

Chapter 3: The Apostles Laid Hands

Chapter 4: As The Father Has Sent Me, I Also Send You

Chapter 5: Ministering Effectively

Chapter 6: Lay Hands Suddenly On No Man

INTRODUCTION

"Afterward he appeared unto the eleven as they sat at meat, and upbraided them with their unbelief and hardness of heart, because they believed not them which had seen him after he was risen. And he said unto them, Go ye into all the world, and preach the gospel to every creature. He that believeth and is baptized shall be saved; but he that believeth not shall be damned. And these signs shall follow them that believe; In my name shall they cast out devils; they shall speak with new tongues; They shall take up serpents; and if they drink any deadly thing, it shall not hurt them; **they shall lay hands on the sick, and they shall recover**" *Mark 16:14-18*

Jesus, whilst rounding up his earthly ministry, gave the Apostles a great task which is commonly called "The Great Commission". He, further, told there were some signs that would follow anyone who believes in Him. Apart from the fact that anyone who believes in Jesus would be saved and not be damned, there were other things that would begin to follow such persons.

These were the signs Jesus said would follow such individual ;

1. They will cast out devils (demons or unclean spirit) in Jesus' name.
2. They will speak with new tongues (they will receive a prayer language).
3. They will be able to take up serpents. (This is divine immunity against Satanic attacks, for we know that

the devil is called serpent, that old dragon – Rev 20:2).

4. Peradventure they drink any deadly thing, they will not be hurt. (This is also called divine immunity).

5. They will lay hands on the sick, and the sick person will recover (This is supernatural ability against sickness, to bring wholeness and wellness unto anyone sick).

Jesus said that all these five major signs will characterize the believer. All he needs to do is believe! The signs, Jesus talked about, can be divided into two; namely, power against satanic works and power for a dynamic prayer life.

I am of the opinion that if Jesus promised the happening of certain things, for or through a believer, would indeed happen. If it does not happen, we are either ignorant of the promise or our belief in God is not strong enough.

The purpose of this book is to show you, amongst many other things, that every believer can and should be able to lay hands on the sick, and also to know how you can achieve better results.

I pray that the Holy Spirit will open the eyes of your understanding and that as you read, the spirit of wisdom and revelation in the knowledge of the Lord will come upon you. I pray that you will see beyond the letters and the Lord will take you into the experience of what he promised would happen when you lay hands.

CHAPTER ONE

The Doctrine of Laying on of Hands

"Of the doctrine of baptisms, and of laying on of hands, and of resurrection of the dead, and of eternal judgment"
Heb 6:2

Certain basic teachings are essential for all believers to understand. These teachings include the importance of faith in God, the foolishness of trying to earn salvation by doing good deeds, understanding what baptisms really means and the different types of baptisms, the comprehension of spiritual gifts (of which laying hands is part of) and the facts of resurrection of the dead, the judgements of both the living and of the dead, and finally, the doctrine of eternal life.

To become mature Christians, we need to move beyond – but not away from – the elementary teachings into the deeper waters of the Christian faith. It is sad that today, in many Christian circles, we major on what the writer of Hebrews referred to as elementary – basic – teachings of the doctrine of Christ. Mature Christians should endeavour to teach new Christians the elementary teachings of the faith.

We are not to discard these basic teachings because they form the foundation of a strong Christian life. I have discovered that many who have been in the Lord for many years are not growing well, or are having challenges believing some basic Bible truth are in this situation because they didn't have a good grasp of the basic teachings, the writer of Hebrews wrote about.

There is a strength that these basic – elementary – teachings produces in you if you are well taught and grounded in it. It will make you progressive and productive in your walk with the Lord.

I think we need to revisit these basic teachings so that men and women in our assemblies are those who are well nourished and sound in the words of faith.

In this chapter, we will consider one of the basic teachings – *The Doctrine of Laying on of Hands.*

The first thought I want to communicate to you is what is a doctrine? A doctrine is a teaching or that which is taught, an instruction, or what is being practiced. In Acts 2:42 we read that, *"...they continued stedfastly in the apostles' doctrine and fellowship, and in breaking of bread, and in prayers"*. Did you notice what they continued in? They continued in the apostles' doctrine. Meaning they continued in the things the apostles taught, they didn't manufacture their own set of teachings.

One of such teachings – doctrine/practice - that we ought to continue in is the laying on of hands.

LAYING ON OF HANDS IN THE OLD TESTAMENT

In the Old Testament, the act of laying on of hands was essentially done, though not exclusive to it, when sin (transgression) was to be dealt with. Hands (of those who had committed a sin) were laid on animals and the animals are sent into the wilderness. What is done here is that the sin of such people is transferred onto the animal and instead of dying for their sin, the animal, which now stands as a sinner will die. In some cases, the animals are to be killed by the appointed priest who will sprinkle the blood on the altar. This is a picture of Jesus as the lamb slain for the sin of the whole world. (See Leviticus 4 &16, Rev 13:8, John 1:29)

Another occasion where we see laying on of hands in the Old Testament is when the Levites were being consecrated and separated on to the service of God (See Numbers 8). We could call this ordination.

When Joshua succeeded Moses, Bible recorded that, *"And Joshua the son of Nun was full of the spirit of wisdom; for Moses had laid his hands upon him: and the children of Israel hearkened unto him, and did as the LORD commanded Moses."* Deut 34:9. (See also Num 27:15-23).

Joshua was filled with the spirit of wisdom because Moses laid hands on him. A new depth, dimension and operation of God began to work in the ministry of Joshua. What was not happening before, will now begin to manifest.

I remember when I celebrated my thirtieth birthday, by divine arrangements; Rev and Rev (Mrs) Areogun was in London. My wife and I met with them, daddy prayed and laid his hands on me and said, *"from now on let the supernatural mark your ministry and let the gifts of the spirit begin to operate as you minister".* Like a switch of light, after that prayer, the manifestation of the spirit became a more regular occurrence in my ministry. I particularly took note of some manifestations that has never occurred during my ministration such as demonic manifestation and casting out devils.

My first encounter with a demon manifesting was after hands were laid on me. I was ministering in a Church at night, it was a prayer meeting, I called out some set of people by the Holy Spirit, and laid hands on them. As soon as I got to this lady it was like a switch, the demon inside her was whistling, sticking out her tongue, speaking mockery and saying all sorts about the lady. It was a strange experience but I could trace that divine working and operation to the fact that it began to happen because hands were laid on me.

The ministry of Joshua will never be the same again because something has been transferred into him. From a Scriptural standpoint, something is transferred when hands are laid on any individual. This is the reason why you must have the right person lay hands on you so that what is transferred into you is not poison. Bishop Oyedepo said when God called him in to the ministry, God said to him, *"I will not have you go as others have gone, I will have hands laid on you so as to befilled with the spirit of wisdom"*

LAYING ON OF HANDS IN THE NEW TESTATMENT

In the New Testament, we see the same practice of laying-on of hands but in a little different manner and with intention. In the New Testament, we do not lay hands on animals for the transference of our sins. Jesus bore it all.

Instances (purposes for which hands) were laid in the New Testament:

1. For Healing and Deliverance: Luke 4:40, Acts 28:8.
2. For the Baptism in the Holy Spirit: Acts 19:6 & Acts 8:16-18.
3. For transference/impartation of spiritual gifts: 1Tim 4:14, 2Tim 1:6.
4. For Ordination: Acts 6:1-6.
5. For Blessing: Mark 10:16.

The above listed are some of the instances in the Bible where hands were laid and the purposes for which they were laid. Laying-on of hands is not an empty practice; it is done to achieve something divine. God has set it so in the Church, we have to align with His purpose.

ESSENTIAL TO EVERY BELIEVER

What you will notice is that when we come into the New Testament, the scope of laying-on of hands seem to increase and becomes a major act or practice within the body of Christ. I want to call your attention to what Paul said to the Church at Rome. He said, *"For I long to see you, that I may impart unto you some spiritual gift, to the end ye may be established;"* Rom 1:11.

Paul wanted to see the brethren in Rome so that he could transfer some spiritual gift unto them. This gift would enable the Church of Rome to be established.

To be established not just as a Church that exists, but to be grounded in their walk with the Lord. This gift would help them be unshakable in the face of life challenges. How will he, then, transfer or impart this gift to them? Let us allow the scripture to answer scriptures. In writing to Timothy, Paul said, "*Wherefore I put thee in remembrance that thou stir up the gift of God, **which is in thee by the putting on of my hands.**"* 2Tim 1:6.

The gift on Timothy that he needed to stir up came on him when Paul laid hands on him. It is safe to conclude that Paul intended to come into the Church in Rome and lay hands on them so as to receive the spiritual gift that will enhance their walk with the Lord. This shows that the doctrine of laying-on of hands is essential to the nourishment and establishment of a believer's spiritual life.

Endeavour to have the right hands (I mean by the right person) laid on you. You will profit from it.

WE LAY HANDS, NOT LEGS

As I bring this chapter to a close, there is a caution we-have to all beware of, either as someone who is laying the hands or as an individual on whom hands are being laid on.

Be reminded that it is the doctrine of laying-on of hands not legs. We are to lay hands on God's people and not legs. Kenneth E. Hagin said Jesus appeared unto him and spoke to him about his ministry when he gave him a peculiar anointing to minister to the sick. He said Jesus put his finger on his hands and told him that when he laid hands, he would detect the presence of evil spirit in a body if they were present and responsible for the affliction, he would be able to cast them out.

He said when Jesus had finished speaking and was about to leave, he told him and said, *"I told you to lay your hands not your legs"*.

This caution had to be given because if you are not properly trained and disciplined, the realm of the anointing is a realm that you might be carried away with. You may be a genuine minister of the gospel but you have been carried away by the euphoria of the anointing and instead of laying hands, you lay your legs. Nothing should move you to a point where you lay your legs on the children of God. This should not happen!

There are many strange happenings today in the body of Christ that should not be present. Many have neglected laying hands and have started laying all kinds of things. Serious attention must be given to this divine instruction – it is laying-on of HANDS!

In fact, despite the fact that we are to lay hands, there are parts of the body a minister laying hands on people should not touch. A male minister should not lay hands on sensitive areas of a female person. If you do this in the name of laying hands, you are stepping out of divine boundaries and the enemy may attack you. Lay hands on the head and the anointing will transfer to any part of the body that might need attention.

I am persuaded that the instruction Jesus gave to Kenneth E. Hagin is still relevant for us today.

CHAPTER TWO

Jesus Laid Hands

"How God anointed Jesus of Nazareth with the Holy Ghost and with power: who went about doing good, and healing all that were oppressed of the devil; for God was with him."
Acts 10:38

We know that Jesus did many miracles during his earthly ministry, but the question is how did they all came about? I discovered that Jesus did about 37 miracles, which were achieved through various means. I did a division myself, I went through all of those miracles and categorised them.

Miracles of Jesus Categorised
1. By the spoken word (See John 4:43-54, Luke 4:31-36, Mat 8:16-17, Mat 8:5-13, Mark 5:1-20, Mat 8:23-37, Mat 21:18-22, John 11:1-45, Mark 3:1-6, Luke 8:40-56, Luke 4:31-36.
2. By Laying-on of hands.
3. By both laying-on of hands and spoken words.
4. By instructions. Here, Jesus is usually seen to give instructions to some individuals, and if obeyed, they received their miracles (See John 2:1-11, Luke 5:1-11, John 5:1-15, John 9:1-12, Luke 17:11-19, John 21:4-11, Mat 17:24-27).
5. By the individual's faith (See Mark 5:25-34, Luke 8:42-48, Mat 14:34-36, Mark 7:24-30).
6.

By this division, we are able to see that God moves and

does his things in different ways. You cannot confine God to a method or a means. He may decide to repeat the method; he may choose to use another. In this case, he may perform a miracle by a spoken word, at another time does the same miracle by laying-on of hands and at another season he may give an instruction. Every believer must be open to the guidance of the Holy Spirit to know the specific thing to be done that will bring about the desired miracle.

MIRACLES THROUGH THE LAYING-ON OF HANDS

We know that laying-on of hands is not an ordinary act, it may look ordinary to the ignorant minds, but acts such as laying on of hands are never to be taken lightly because of what is being transferred. Whenever hands are laid on you something happens, especially if it's directed by the Holy Spirit. In the earthly ministry of Jesus, He laid hands on different people for different reasons and we know that some things happened. I will point out the instances where Jesus laid hands on people and the resultant effect.

Bible says that Jesus was anointed with the Holy Spirit and power; he went about doing good and healing all that were oppressed of the devil. One of the means through which the power of God flowed to heal the oppressed was by the laying-on of hands. If you will be used by God to deliver the oppressed, you must never be afraid of laying hands on people. I have had personal experiences where, when I laid hands on some individuals that they received their freedom.

Few instances where Jesus laid hands on the oppressed:

1.   Jesus Heals Peter's Mother-in-Law Sick With Fever: Mat 8:14-15. *"And when Jesus was come into Peter's house, he saw his wife's mother laid, and sick of a fever. And he touched her hand, and the fever left her: and she arose, and ministered unto them."* Peter's mother-in-law had been sick with fever for a while but when she came in contact with Jesus, the fever left! How did it go? Bible says Jesus touched her. It is possible that Jesus spoke to the fever, but we know that he touched her!

2.   At Evening, Jesus Healed Many That Were Oppressed: Luke 4:40-42. *"Now when the sun was setting, all they that had any sick with divers diseases brought them unto him; and he laid his hands on every one of them, and healed them. And devils also came out of many, crying out, and saying, Thou art Christ the Son of God. And he rebuking them suffered them not to speak: for they knew that he was Christ. And when it was day, he departed and went into a desert place: and the people sought him, and came unto him, and stayed him, that he should not depart from them"* After Jesus left the house of Peter, somehow words got around about him and many brought their sick to him so as to heal them. Did you notice what Jesus did? Bible says, **"he laid his hands on every one of them, and healed them"** As he laid hands, it was also recorded that Demons came out of many people. So, either his presence, his words, or the hand that was laid eject

led the demon. Many times, in the Bible, where we see people healed of many diseases, we often saw that demons, or evil spirits had to be expelled from the people. This means that many sicknesses and diseases were a result of evil spirit – one way or the other. Later on, I will elaborate this a little more.

3.   Jesus Cleanses a Man With Leprosy: Mat 8:1-4. *"When he was come down from the mountain, great multitudes followed him. And, behold, there came a leper and worshipped him, saying, Lord, if thou wilt, thou canst make me clean. And Jesus put forth his hand, and touched him, saying, I will; be thou clean. And immediately his leprosy was cleansed. And Jesus saith unto him, See thou tell no man; but go thy way, shew thyself to the priest, and offer the gift that Moses commanded, for a testimony unto them".* You cannot separate compassion from the healing anointing. Every minister of God who has carried the healing ministry successfully is a compassionate person. It takes a level of compassion to touch a man with leprosy (given the scare of contamination). We see Jesus, here again, bringing healing to a man with a disease no one wants to associate with. (I am fully persuaded that it is God's will to heal every one of their diseases and pain). The man said to Jesus that, *"if thou wilt, thou canst make me clean."* I love Jesus' response, **"And Jesus put forth his hand, and touched him,** *saying, I will; be thou clean. And immediately his leprosy was cleansed"* Jesus is still in the business of cleansing today!

4.   Jesus Raises Jairus' Daughter Back to Life: Mat 9:18, 23-25. What we notice, here, is that Jairus himself

requested that Jesus would come and lay hands on her dying daughter (See Mark 5:23). That means, somehow, Jairus knew the importance of laying-on of hands and believed in it. He knew that life will be transmitted. We do not know how he came about this wonderful insight, which eventually gave him back his daughter from death. *"While he spake these things unto them, behold, there came a certain ruler, and worshipped him, saying, My daughter is even now dead: but come and lay thy hand upon her, and she shall live"* Did you notice that? Come and lay *THY HAND UPON HER AND SHE SHALL LIVE*. In other words, I know that if you can lay your hands on her, she will live. *"And when Jesus came into the ruler's house, and saw the minstrels and the people making a noise, He said unto them, Give place: for the maid is not dead, but sleepeth. And they laughed him to scorn. But when the people were put forth, he went in, and took her by the hand, and the maid arose."*

5.　　Jesus Heals Two Blind Men: Mat 9:27-31. *"And when Jesus departed thence, two blind men followed him, crying, and saying, Thou son of David, have mercy on us. And when he was come into the house, the blind men came to him: and Jesus saith unto them, Believe ye that I am able to do this? They said unto him, Yea, Lord. Then touched he their eyes, saying, According to your faith be it unto you"* The significant thing I want you to notice here is that Jesus didn't
ay his hands on these blind men upon seeing them. He did when he got them into a position where they could receive the healing they needed. Notice that Jesus said to them *BELIEVE YE THAT I AM ABLE TO DO THIS?*

He said it to ascertain if they really believe. Not everyone seeking for healing and deliverance believes that they will receive it indeed.

6. Jesus Heals a Blind Man at Bethsaida: Mark 8:22-25. *"And he cometh to Bethsaida; and they bring a blind man unto him, and besought him to touch him. And he took the blind man by the hand, and led him out of the town; and when he had spit on his eyes, and put his hands upon him, he asked him if he saw ought. And he looked up, and said, I see men as trees, walking. After that he put his hands again upon his eyes, and made him look up: and he was restored, and saw every man clearly."* Here again, we see another instance where a demand is made for Jesus' hands to be laid on a sick fellow. Bible says, "...and besought him to touch him" The word besought is from the Greek word *Parakaleho* which means to beg, implore, desire, entreat, and call for. In other words, Jesus was desperately called upon to touch this man. This is to show you that wholeness and wellness can be brought to the sick if it comes in contact with God's power through the laying-on of hands. John Graham Lake said that the healing power of God is tangible. You know it when it's in operation! Jesus did something to this man that is not recorded anywhere else in the Bible – he touched him twice! He laid hands on his eyes twice. The first touch didn't bring about the desired result, though it accomplished something because we know he was blind but could at least sea men as tree after the first laying-on of hands. Because what the man needed was a perfect restoration of his sight, which the first laying-on of hands didn't accomplish, a second touch was essent

ial. What is the lesson here for anyone who will administer God's healing power? Never be tired of laying hands until you get the desired result. Some may not need a second touch, they might just need to work out their own faith to get the victory, certainly, others might need numerous touches.

7.   Jesus Heals a Woman with the spirit of Infirmity: Luke 13:10-16. *"And he was teaching in one of the synagogues on the sabbath. And, behold, there was a woman which had a spirit of infirmity eighteen years, and was bowed together, and could in no wise lift up herself. And when Jesus saw her, he called her to him, and said unto her, Woman, thou art loosed from thine infirmity. And he laid his hands on her: and immediately she was made straight, and glorified God. And the ruler of the synagogue answered with indignation, because that Jesus had healed on the sabbath day, and said unto the people, There are six days in which men ought to work: in them therefore come and be healed, and not on the sabbath day. The Lord then answered him, and said, Thou hypocrite, doth not each one of you on the sabbath loose his ox or his ass from the stall, and lead him away to watering? And ought not this woman, being a daughter of Abraham, whom Satan hath bound, lo, these eighteen years, be loosed from this bond on the sabbath day?* This woman had a terrible physiological condition that is not ordinary. It was a result of satanic bondage through a spirit of infirmity. Medical doctors couldn't have helped because there is no medical solution to satanic infirmity! Jesus saw this woman; he called her to him and said *unto her woman, thou art loosed from thin infirmity.* Jesus did not stop

there, he proceeded to lay hands on her, at this point, Bible says immediately she was made straight and glorified God. My question is, when was she made straight? IMMEDIATELY HANDS WERE LAID ON HER! The spoken word is good, Jesus did many of his miracles through the spoken word. However, in some circumstances, he went further and touched the people. You might need to do the same.

CHAPTER THREE

THE APOSTLES LAY HANDS

"And by the hands of the apostles were many signs and wonders wrought among the people; (and they were all with one accord in Solomon's porch."
Acts 5:12

In the previous chapter, I showed us some of the instances where Jesus laid hands on people and what the results were. In this chapter, I will look at laying-on of hands in the ministry of some of the apostles.

Jesus set a pattern of ministry for them and they emulated what they saw. You should look through the Bible, and do what you see in there, it may not be widely accepted, but if Jesus did it, you can also do it.

The ministry of the apostles was marked with signs and wonders just as the ministry of Jesus was. Bible says, *"...by the hands of the apostles were many signs and wonders wrought among the people..."* Acts 5:12. Did you notice it says BY THE HANDS OF THE APOSTLES? This means many signs and wonders will be done through the hands of believers if we are ready for the master's speaking in tongues, for we read that, *"...when Simon saw t* use.

Let's see some of the many signs and wonders that God did through the hands of the apostles

HEALING OF A LAME MAN – Acts 3:1-9

"Now Peter and John went up together into the tem-

ple at the hour of prayer, being the ninth hour. And a certain man lame from his mother's womb was carried, whom they laid daily at the gate of the temple which is called Beautiful, to ask alms of them that entered into the temple; Who seeing Peter and John about to go into the temple asked an alms. And Peter, fastening his eyes upon him with John, said, Look on us. And he gave heed unto them, expecting to receive something of them. Then Peter said, Silver and gold have I none; but such as I have give I thee: In the name of Jesus Christ of Nazareth rise up and walk. And he took him by the right hand, and lifted him up: and immediately his feet and ankle bones received strength. And he leaping up stood, and walked, and entered with them into the temple, walking, and leaping, and praising God. And all the people saw him walking and praising God:"

Bible says this man had been born lame from his mother's womb. Because of this affliction, he had asked for alms before he could eat. Peter and John saw him one day and his life was changed. *"Then Peter said, Silver and gold have I none; but such as I have give I thee: In the name of Jesus Christ of Nazareth rise up and walk. And he took him by the right hand, and lifted him up:"* Peter spoke a word by faith to this man, I believe the word Peter spoke released the power of God, but the manifestation of that power was not evident until, *"...he(Peter) took him by the right hand, and lifted him up:..."* When he did this, Bible says, *"...and immediately his feet and ankle bones received strength. And he leaping up stood, and walked..."* Immediately after Peter took him by the right hand, his ankle bones received strength. You don't take something with your legs, neither do you use your head. You take with the hands. That means Peter laid hands on him to take him up.

What you will notice, here, is that one of the channels of releasing the manifestation of God's power, i.e. for making the power of God visible is, by laying-on of hands.

PETER AND JOHN MINISTERED THE HOLY SPIRIT – Acts 8:14-18

"Now when the apostles which were at Jerusalem heard that Samaria had received the word of God, they sent unto them Peter and John: Who, when they were come down, prayed for them, that they might receive the Holy Ghost: (For as yet he was fallen upon none of them: only they were baptized in the name of the Lord Jesus.) Then laid they their hands on them, and they received the Holy Ghost. And when Simon saw that through laying on of the apostles' hands the Holy Ghost was given, he offered them money"

A revival had started in the city of Samaria through the ministry of Philip the Evangelist. He got them saved and baptised in water. He did many signs and wonder as we read that, "Then Philip went down to the city of Samaria, and preached Christ unto them. And the people with one accord gave heed unto those things which Philip spake, hearing and seeing the miracles which he did. For unclean spirits, crying with loud voice, came out of many that were possessed with them: and many taken with palsies, and that were lame, were healed." Acts 8:5-7.

Though all that happened through his ministry, it excluded the Holy Ghost baptism with the evidence of speaking in tongues. *"when the apostles which were at Jerusalem heard that Samaria had received the word of God, they sent unto them Peter and John: Who, when they were come down, prayed for them, that they might receive the Holy Ghost"*. When the apostles came, they prayed for the Samaritan to receive the Holy Ghosts and the apostles did something more, Bible says, *"...Then laid they their (apostles) hands on them (Samaritans), and they received the Holy Ghost.*

By the laying-on of the apostle's hands, we see that the Holy Spirit baptism was imparted with the evidence of *hat through laying on of the apostles' hands the Holy Ghost was given, he offered them money"*. Something visible happened to the Samaritans when hands were laid on them.

PAUL MINISTERED THE HOLY SPIRIT BAPTISM – Acts 19:1-6.

"And it came to pass, that, while Apollos was at Corinth, Paul having passed through the upper coasts came to Ephesus: and finding certain disciples, He said unto them, Have ye received the Holy Ghost since ye believed? And they said unto him, We have not so much as heard whether there be any Holy Ghost. And he said unto them, Unto what then were ye baptized? And they said, Unto John's baptism. Then said Paul, John verily baptized with the baptism of repentance, saying unto the people, that they should believe on him which should come after him, that is, on Christ Jesus. When they heard this, they were baptized in the name of the Lord Jesus. And when Paul had laid his

hands upon them, the Holy Ghost came on them; and they spake with tongues, and prophesied."

Here we see Paul ministering the baptism of the Holy Spirit to disciples at Ephesus. He did this through the laying-on of hands. Paul asked, *"Have ye received the Holy Ghost since ye believed...?"* Afterwards, Paul, *"laid his hands upon them, the Holy Ghost came on them; and they spake with tongues, and prophesied."* There are different ways an individual may receive the baptism of the Holy Spirit with evidence of speaking in tongues. One of such definite avenues is by laying-on of hands.

SPECIAL MIRACLES –HEALING AND DELIVERANCES - BY THE HANDS OF PAUL – Acts 19:11-12.

"And God wrought special miracles by the hands of Paul: So that from his body were brought unto the sick handkerchiefs or aprons, and the diseases departed from them, and the evil spirits went out of them"

The Modern English Version of the Bible puts Acts 19:11-12 like this, "God worked powerful miracles by the hands of Paul. So handkerchiefs or aprons he had touched were brought to the sick, and the diseases left them, and the evil spirits went out of them"

God did many things – signs and wonders – through the apostles. A miracle, in itself, is special because you are bringing the power of God into a situation. You are bringing the supernatural into the natural. However, Bible also said that God did *"Special Miracles"* through the hands of Paul. It is safe to say that God gave Paul what we could call a "Special Anointing". I imagine that special miracles would be a result of special anointing. What were these special miracles that God did through the hands of Paul? *"So handkerchiefs or aprons he had touched were brought to the sick, and the diseases left them, and the evil spirits went out of them"*

Paul laid hands on clothing materials such as handkerchiefs and aprons, these materials were then passed on to the sick and the Bible says, *"...the diseases left them, and the evil spirits went out of them"*. The diseases and evil spirits had to leave because it came in contact with material that had an unusual anointing on it. We see this also in the earthly ministry of Jesus, a woman with the issue of blood touched the hem of Jesus' garment and Bible says, *"And straightway the fountain of her blood was dried up, and she felt in her body that she was healed of that plague."* (See Mark5:25-34). The flow of blood dried up immediately she made contact with Jesus' garment. In fact, Jesus said, *"... Who touched me? When all denied, Peter and they, that were with him said, Master, the multitude throng thee and press thee, and sayest thou, Who touched me? And Jesus said, Somebody hath touched me: for I perceive that virtue is gone out of me"* Luke 8:45-46.

Jesus said he perceived that virtue had gone out of him. The word translated VIRTUE is from the Greek word DUNAMIS which means POWER or according to Strong's Bible MIRACULOUS POWER! This same power came out from the materials Paul had touched and it resulted into healing and deliverance.

PECULIAR/SPECIAL ANOINTING

Speaking about this kind of "*Special or Peculiar Anointing*", I believe they are still present in the body of Christ. I wrote in chapter one how Kenneth E. Hagin said Jesus appeared to him on 2nd of September 1950 and gave him a special anointing to minister to the sick.

Oral Robert, in his autobiography – *Expect A Miracle, My Life And Ministry* – said that after he fulfilled some instructions given to him by the Lord. The Lord said to him "*From this hour you shall have My power to heal the sick and to cast out demons.*"

He wrote about another encounter he had during a service in Nowata, Oklahoma. He said he heard the voice of God say to him, "*Son, you have been faithful to this hour, and now you will feel My presence in your right hand. Through My presence, you will be able to detect the presence of demons. You will know their number and name, and will have My power to cast them out*"

This is God bringing Oral into a phase in his ministry where a special anointing will begin to operate through him. At the first encounter, he would have God's power to heal the sick and cast out demons. This, every believer can do or should be able to do. But the second encounter is specific and deeper than the first. In the second, he would detect the presence of demons, feel God's power in his right hand, know the name and numbers of demons present and then cast them out.

Having been involved in the ministry for some time, my personal experience is that, when you operate more in the gifts of the Holy Spirit – especially the discerning of spirit - healings and deliverances are easily achieved.

Every believer can lay hands on the sick by obeying the scriptures. God will honour such acts of faith and obedience, however, there are those with such peculiar ministries like that of Oral Roberts and Kenneth Hagin, whom Jesus – the head of the Church – had called and anointed with the healing power. These sets of anointing will get more results than a believer who is obeying Mark 16:17-18, *"And these signs shall follow them that believe; In my name shall they…. they shall lay hands on the sick, and they shall recover"*

Does that mean we should wait until we are anointed like Oral Roberts and Kenneth Hagin? No! I believe this kind of special anointing is given as a result of faithfulness with the small or initial measure, grace or anointing they started with (See Luke 16:10). As a believer, you should start from wherever you are, minister according to the level of your faith and God will reward and increase you.

PAUL HEALS THE FATHER OF PUBLIUS AND OTHERS
– Acts 28:7-9

"In the same quarters were possessions of the chief man of the island, whose name was Publius; who received us, and lodged us three days courteously. And it came to pass, that the father of Publius lay sick of a fever and of a bloody flux: to whom Paul entered in, and prayed, and laid his hands on him, and healed

him. So when this was done, others also, which had diseases in the island, came, and were healed"

Paul had a shipwreck on his way to Rome and was forced to stop at the Island of Malta, upon arriving; the leader of the island – Publius - received them well. However, Publius' father was ill with fever and dysentery. When Paul heard, he went and prayed for him to be healed by laying hands on him. When Paul laid hands on Publius' father, miraculous power – DUNAMIS – went through his hands, and that power healed him.

The healing God wrought through the laying-on of hands of apostle Paul got around, as Bible says, *"… others also, which had diseases in the island, came, and were healed"*. Others, who were sick, came and were healed. Paul would have prayed and laid hands on them.

In concluding this chapter, we have seen that the laying-on of hands played a major role in the signs and wonders God did through the ministry of the apostles. We know that God can and does work in different ways, however, laying-on of hands remains a doctrine which believers should xercise so as to see the manifestation of God's power.

CHAPTER FOUR

AS THE FATHER HAS SENT ME, I ALSO SEND YOU

"Then said Jesus to them again, Peace be unto you: as my Father hath sent me, even so send I you."
John 20:21

We are to do the works of Christ. We are to imitate what he did during his earthly ministry. That is why studying the earthly ministry of Jesus is mandatory for anyone who wishes to replicate what the master did.

Oral Robert said he decided to preach and teach like Jesus did. He said he had to read the four gospels and the book of Acts of the Apostles many time before he could function in a particular anointing. In fact, that was open the door to his healing ministry.

In the Bible, you will find the Apostles ministering like Jesus did. Jesus was their example, so they followed him and did things in the way and manner that he did. Peter walked on water because he saw Jesus did it (See Mat 14:25-29).

PETER RAISES THE DEAD LIKE JESUS

In the book of Acts of the Apostle, we see how Peter raised a woman who had died back to life (See Acts 9:36-42). "But Peter put them all forth (sent them out), and kneeled down, and prayed; and turning him to the body said, Tabitha, arise. And she opened her eyes: and when she saw Peter, she sat up"
It is clear that Peter simply repeated what he saw Jesus

did when he raised different people from the dead (See Mark 5:40). Peter sent everyone away just like Jesus did. There is no point reinventing the wheel.

CAUTION

Though we are to do the works of Jesus – replicate what he did. We are to do it under the leadership of the Holy Spirit. You have to be led. Remember Jesus, *"… said unto them, Verily, verily, I say unto you, THE SON CAN DO NOTHING OF HIMSELF, BUT WHAT HE SEETH THE FATHER DO: FOR WHAT THINGS SOEVER HE DOETH, THESE ALSO DOETH THE SON LIKEWISE. For the Father loveth the Son, and sheweth him all things that himself doeth: and he will shew him greater works than these, that ye may marvel.* John 5:19-20.

We are to do *WHAT WE SEE THE FATHER DOING*. Never do anything to prove anything to anyone, make sure you are fully persuaded to minister in the way you do.

CHAPTER 5

MINISTERING EFFECTIVELY

"Nevertheless the foundation of God standeth sure, having this seal, The Lord knoweth them that are his. AND, LET EVERY ONE THAT NAMETH THE NAME OF CHRIST DEPART FROM INIQUITY. But in a great house there are not only vessels of gold and of silver, but also of wood and of earth; and some to honour, and some to dishonour. IF A MAN THEREFORE PURGE HIMSELF FROM THESE, HE SHALL BE A VESSEL UNTO HONOUR, SANCTIFIED, AND MEET FOR THE MASTER'S USE, AND PREPARED UNTO EVERY GOOD WORK". **2Tim 2:19-21.**

God is willing and ready to use you more than you are ready to be used. I don't think it is appropriate to pray that God should use you, rather, pray for God to make you useable! When you come to the place where you are useable, you will realise that there is work waiting for you to be done. Jesus said, *"... The harvest truly is great, but the labourers are few: pray ye therefore the Lord of the harvest, that he would send forth labourers into his harvest."* Luke 10:2.

Charles Finney said that he realised that there was an anointing that rested on his words when he spoke to sinners about salvation. He said many of them got saved. However, he realised that at some point the anointing on his words was low (he probably knew this by the spirit or by the evident results he saw), he said that whenever this is the case, he would go on a three day fasting and prayer. He said every time he did it, the anointing gets restored as it were.

For a child of God, there are activities that increase the grace of God on him/her. Some of these activities are daily, some weekly, monthly and perhaps yearly. These activities make the person *READY FOR THE MASTER'S USE, AND PREPARED UNTO EVERY GOOD WORK.*

In this chapter, I want to look at some of the things a believer should do in order to help him become more effective in the work of the Lord. Paul called it *BEING FIT FOR THE MASTER'S USE AND PREPARED UNTO EVERY GOOD WORK.* Before the master makes use of you, you have to first be prepared. Esther didn't become a queen overnight; she had to be prepared for it (See Esther 1 & 2). You can't hold or maintain a position for a longer period of time, you have not been prepared for!

One area the master wants to use us in, is the ministry of laying-on of hands. You will agree with me that this is a good work. Paul said we should be *PREPARED UNTO EVERY GOOD WORK.* You notice he said *EVERY GOOD WORK*, which means there are many good works. Laying-on of hands is just one of such.

PRACTICAL ACTIVITIES THAT ENHANCES EFFECTIVE LAYING-ON OF HANDS:

The Bible is filled with instructions that if obeyed, will make you more effective in laying-on of hands. We will look at some of them.

DEPART FROM INIQUITY
Paul told Timothy, "*...The Lord knoweth them that are his. And, LET EVERY ONE THAT NAMETH THE NAME OF CHRIST DEPART FROM INIQUITY*" 2Tim 2:19. *This means,*

"All who belong to the LORD must turn away from evil" (NLT). *"Everyone who names the name of the Lord must abstain from unrighteousness."* (Lexham English Bible). You must turn away from evil, to be involved in evil and do ministry is to open up yourself for attacks from the Devil.

<u>PURGE YOURSELF</u> (2Tim 3:16-17; 1Thess 4:1-7).
"If a man therefore purge himself from these, he shall be a vessel unto honour, sanctified, and meet for the master's use, and prepared unto every good work" 2Tim 2:21. "Purge" is from the Greek word, "EKKATHAI-RO" which means to thoroughly clean"

Paul is, therefore, saying that a man who will minister effectively must clean himself THOROUGHLY! What should he clean himself from? Paul said, *"But in a great house there are not only vessels of gold and of silver, but also of wood and of earth; and some to honour, AND SOME TO DISHONOUR"* 2Tim 2:20. He should clean himself thoroughly from whatever is dishonouring!

You must ensure that you purge yourself thoroughly before laying hands on people because if you don't, you may transfer onto them what you didn't intend. You see, when hands are laid, you don't only transfer the anointing, you may transfer something else, which may not be good.

John Graham Lake said he was in a city and was sick, so he needed someone to pray for him, a man was present who laid hands on him and prayed as he knelt down, he said he arose from that place with one of the most tremendous passions in his nature – one of the most terrible conditions of sensuousness. He said latter, the man who laid hands on him came to confess of a particular character in his life. John G. Lake said he knew he received of the vileness of the person in his own nature. He said it took days before he felt holy and pure in the sight of God.

If you possess in your nature some sort of vileness – inordinate/unscriptural affection – do not lay hands on anyone. You will transfer some of such vileness to whoever you lay your hands on.

STUDY

Everyone God called (especially kings), he required that they read the book of the law – 5 books of Moses – so that they will function effectively. In Deuteronomy 17, we see some of the governing principles of kingship in Israel, studying the book of the law was one of it. *"When you come to the land which the LORD your God is giving you, and possess it and dwell in it, and say, 'I will set a king over me like all the nations that are around me,' 15 you shall surely set a king over you whom the LORD your God chooses; one from among your brethren you shall set as king over you; you may not set a foreigner over you, who is not your brother. 16 But he shall not multiply horses for himself, nor causethe people to return to Egypt to multiply horses, for the LORD has said to you, 'You shall not return that way again.' 17 Neither shall he multiply wives for himself, lest his heart turn away; nor shall he greatly multiply silver and gold for himself.* "ALSO IT SHALL BE, WHEN HE SITS ON THE THRONE OF HIS KINGDOM, THAT HE SHALL WRITE FOR HIMSELF A COPY OF THIS LAW IN A BOOK, FROM THE ONE BEFORE THE PRIESTS, THE LEVITES. AND IT SHALL BE WITH HIM, AND H**E SHALL READ IT ALL THE DAYS OF HIS LIFE**, THAT HE MAY LEARN TO FEAR THE LORD HIS

GOD AND BE CAREFUL TO OBSERVE ALL THE WORDS OF THIS LAW AND THESE STATUTES, [20] that his heart may not be lifted above his brethren, that he may not turn aside from the commandment to the right hand or to the left, and that he may prolong his days in his kingdom, he and his children in the midst of Israel." V14-20NKJV. He is to read all the days of his life – this means he must develop a studious life. All the kings who did not obey this were either cut short from reigning or not effective (evil reigned in their tenure).

There is no effective ministry without a studious life. Rev Areogun once said, *"If your study is shallow, your ministry is narrow".*

Joshua was told, *"This book of the law shall not depart out of thy mouth; but thou shalt meditate therein day and night, that thou mayest observe to do according to all that is written therein: for then thou shalt make thy way prosperous, and then thou shalt have good success"* Josh 1:8. To make your way prosperous and to have a good success simply means you are effective.

Daniel said he had an understanding by reading books, *"In the first year of his reign I Daniel understood by books the number of the years, whereof the word of the LORD came to Jeremiah the prophet, that he would accomplish seventy years in the desolations of Jerusalem."* Dan 9:2. One of the benefits of reading is that your understanding on that particular subject will increase. When there is understanding, doing/practicing becomes easier.

In the New Testament, Paul told Timothy, *"Study and do your best to present yourself to God approved, a workman [tested by trial] who has no reason to be* ashamed, ACCURATELY HANDLING AND SKILLFULLY TEACHING THE WORD OF TRUTH." 2Tim 2:15AMP.

Accuracy and skilfulness are produced when you devote yourself to studying. You will know how to ACCURATELY HANDLE AND SKILLFULLY TEACH THE WORD OF TRUTH. Or better still, you will become more skilful and accurate in laying hands on people. That means you will get more done, as compared to if you never studied. From personal experience, there are things I know how to do now from reading a book. I remember reading Kenneth Hagin's book - SEVEN STEPS TO RECEIVING THE HOLY SPIRIT. In that book, he gave a systematic way of ministering the Holy Spirit with evidence of speaking in tongue to people who are to be baptised.

I studied it very well, and when the opportunity came, Idid what I read and it happened like he said it would. There are many things I have seen from reading books. It was one of Kenneth Hagin's books from which I learnt that you must not lay legs on any person (though Bible also said we are to lay hands). We are commanded to lay hands; you can't say the spirit told me to lay my legs. I have practiced this since I read it.

As you study the Bible, you may discover that the way and manner you minister may change because you either saw what you were doing that were wrong, or you saw what you were not doing that you ought to do. Or you see something in the Bible that reinforces the way you minister.

PRAY AND FAST REGULARLY

Praying and fasting regularly will help you to minister more effectively. Every preacher knows he can't preach his best on a full stomach! Jesus said, *"And he spake a parable unto them to this end, that men ought always to pray, and not to faint;"* Luke 18:1. Paul said, *"Pray without ceasing."* 1 Thess 5:17.

This is where speaking in tongues comes in; I found it to be very rewarding, effective and productive. John G. Lake was once asked what the secrets of his ministry were. His answer was simple! He said it is speaking in tongues, that is where I get the words I speak to you.

Paul said, *"I thank my God, I speak with tongues more than ye all:"* 1 Cor 14:18. *"Praying always with all prayer and supplication in the Spirit"* Eph 6:18. Spend time praying in tongues, it will make you be more effective.

Earlier in chapter three, I mentioned about Kenneth Hagin, how the Lord called him and gave him a peculiar ministry of laying-on of hands. He said when he waited on the Lord in praying and fasting the sameanointing comes on him again.

MINISTER WITH LOVE AND COMPASSION
"When Jesus heard of it, he departed thence by ship into a desert place apart: and when the people had heard thereof, they followed him on foot out of the cities, And Jesus went forth, and saw a great multitude, AND WAS MOVED WITH COMPASSION TOWARD THEM, AND HE HEALED THEIR SICK." Mat 14:13-14.

Many signs and wonders followed the ministry of Jesus, this was because he had compassion –mercy – on those, he ministered to (See Mat 20:34, Mark 1:40-41). You can't minister effectively if you don't love those you have been sent to. A pastor can't give his best to i his congregation if he doesn't love them.

COMPARING WHAT PAUL AND JESUS SAID

We have seen the context in which Paul was writing, it was that of leadership appointment. Timothy was not to be in a hurry, he was to do it carefully, thoughtfully and most importantly, prayerfully.

However, the context which Jesus spoke was different. It was solely referring to healing the sick. He said t believers should lay hands on the sick and they will recover. Having said that, I believe that a believer should also be careful on how he lays hands. He must be led by the Spirit.

The Holy Spirit may refrain a believer from laying hands on a person for reasons best known to Him (Holy Spirit), which He may tell or not tell the believer. Derek Prince said that he and his friends once laid hands on a particular person who suffered from severe depression; he said later they were all attacked by the same spirit of depression. He said the reason they were attacked by this spirit was that they were not really led by God.

There are some things which we know is the will of God but you may not be permitted to do it by God. For example, the Great Commission is the will of God. We are to preach the gospel to everybody on the earth, but we see instances where the Holy Spirit doesn't allow the apostle to preach.

Let's look at an example in the book of Acts of he Apostles. This was in the ministry of Paul. Bible says, *"Now when they had gone throughout Phrygia and the region of Galatia, AND WERE FORBIDDEN OF THE HOLY GHOST TO PREACH THE WORD IN ASIA, AFTER THEY WERE COME TO MYSIA, THEY ASSAYED TO GO INTO BITHYNIA: BUT THE SPIRIT SUFFERED THEM NOT."*

Acts 16:6-7.

Did you notice the phrase "were forbidden of the Holy Ghost to preach the word in Asia" The question is, does Asia not need the word of God? My answers, the Holy Spirit, who knows the mind of God said that the apostles should not go there! Also, by the Holy Spirit, they were not allowed to go to Bithynia.

This is a proof that what is written in the word of God might be forbidden to a person by the Holy Spirit for reasons best known to him. Other apostles or preachers may want to go to Asia and Bithynia, and the Holy Spirit may approve it.

When it comes to laying-on of hands, in order to safeguard ourselves and avoid spiritual contamination, we must be led by the Holy Spirit.

PRAYER FOR SALVATION

Except a man is born again he will never and can never see the kingdom of God. Salvation is mandatory for anyone that desires to enter into the kingdom of God. Without salvation, no man will see God. You need to be saved from the wrath of God that is coming upon this disobedient generation. Please pray like this . . . . . .

Heavenly father, I come to You in the name of Your Son Jesus. Your word says that, *"And it shall come to pass, that whosoever shall call on the name of the Lord be saved".* Act 2:21. I am calling on you now. I pray and desire that you come into my heart now and be my Lord and Saviour according to your word which says, *"That if thou shalt confess with thy mouth the Lord Jesus, and shalt believe in thine heart that God hath raised him from the dead, thou shalt be saved. For with the heart man believeth unto righteousness;, and with the mouth confession is made unto salvation".* Romans 10:9-10. I do that now, I believe in my heart that Jesus Christ died for me and was raised from the dead on the third day. I confess with my mouth that he is Lord. I ask that you forgive me of my sins and cleanse me with your blood. This I ask for in Jesus name. Amen

We believe you have been saved. Look for a bible believing and teaching church that will enhance your growth in the knowledge and grace of God.

PRAYER FOR THE BAPTISM IN THE HOLY GHOST

Power is needed to run the race which you have just begun. Jesus Christ told His disciples never to go out and do anything until they have been endued with power. The power is made available by the ministry of the Holy Spirit with an evidence of speaking in tongues. God desires that you should be baptized and speak in the heavenly language. The Holy Spirit will give you the utterance but you will have to open your mouth and speak out boldly. You do not have to understand what the words mean just say it out as you receive it. Please pray like this:

Father Lord, I come to you in the name of Jesus Christ and I ask you to fill me with the Holy Spirit now with the evidence of speaking with tongues, because you said in your word that, " . . . If ye then, being evil, know how to give good gifts unto your children: how much more shall your heavenly Father give the Holy Spirit to them that ask him . . . .". Luke 11:13. I also know from your word that, ". . . everyone who asks receives, and he who seeks finds, and to him who knocks it will be opened . . . " Mathew 7:8NKJV. Holy Spirit rise up within me now as I begin to praise God. I am ready and fully expect to speak in tongues now as You give me utterance in the name of Jesus Christ. Amen. Now lift up your hands and begin to praise God then speak those words as they come to you now in Jesus name. Amen

Having received the baptism of the Holy Ghost with the edence of speaking in tongues you must constantly speak in your prayer language.

ABOUT THE BOOK

And these signs shall follow them that believe; In my name shall they cast out devils; they shall speak with new tongues; They shall take up serpents; and if they drink any deadly thing, it shall not hurt them; they shall lay hands on the sick, and they shall recover" Mark 16:14-18

Jesus, whilst rounding up his earthly ministry, gave the Apostles a great task which is commonly called "The Great Commission". He, further, told that there were some signs that would follow anyone who believes in Him. Apart from the fact that anyone who believes in Jesus would be saved and not be damned, there were other things that would begin to follow such people.
These were the signs Jesus said would follow such individual –
1.   They will cast out devils (demons or unclean spirit) in Jesus' name.
2.   They will speak with new tongues (they will receive a prayer language).
3.   They will be able to take up serpents. (This is divine immunity against satanic attacks, for we know that the devil is called serpent, that old dragon – Rev 20:2).
4.   Peradventure they drink any deadly thing, they will not be hurt. (This is also called divine immunity).
5.   They will lay hands on the sick, and the sick person will recover. (This is supernatural ability against sickness, to bring wholeness and wellness unto anyone sick)

ABOUT THE AUTHOR

Ayodeji D. Olusanmi is a teacher and a preacher of the gospel. A dynamic pastor of a branch of Mountain of Fire and Miracle Ministries – the United Kingdom. He studied in the UK as a Biomedical Scientist. He is the author of *The Prayer that Works, The Testimony of a Youth, The Just Shall Live By Faith, Godly Wisdom for Success at the Workplace, Nothing Shall By Any Means Hurt You, They Shall Speak With New Tongues, Lessons from My Father*. He is married to Margaret and they are blessed with beautiful children.

www.ingramcontent.com/pod-product-compliance
Lightning Source LLC
LaVergne TN
LVHW012129070526
838202LV00056B/5929